MW01282338

Top 10 Reasons
to Read the Bible Today

The Life-Changing Benefits
of Daily Bible Reading

Wayne Davies

Get free Bible reading tips at
www.GodWroteTheBook.com

Top 10 Reasons to Read the Bible Today:
The Life-Changing Benefits of Daily Bible Reading

Copyright © 2015, 2019 by Wayne Davies

Learn more information at:
www.GodWroteTheBook.com

Table of Contents

Why I Wrote This Book

Thank you for taking time to read this book. Let me share my thoughts on why I wrote it.

I wrote this book because over the past 40+ years I've had a love/hate relationship with the Bible. And this love/hate relationship with the Bible is simply a reflection of the love/hate relationship I've had with God the Father and His Son Jesus Christ.

Let me explain.

Here's the story of my life in a nutshell, from the standpoint of my relationship to God:

Ages 15-25: Love for God and His Word

I don't remember having much exposure to Christianity until age 15. I heard the gospel as a teenager by attending a Bible-believing church with a good friend and his family. I made a profession of faith in Christ as Savior and was baptized. And I started to read and study the Bible with great zeal.

As high school graduation neared, I felt compelled to enter the ministry, so I studied the Bible as much as I could in college and seminary to prepare for full-time Christian service.

Ages 26-46: Hatred for God and His Word

After entering the ministry as an Assistant Pastor of an evangelical church, my world fell apart. I started having doubts about the faith. Those doubts grew into a full-blown compulsion to walk away from my job and the Christian faith. I wanted out. So I left Jesus and wandered far away from Him, His people and His Word.

Why did I do a thing like that? Short answer: sin. Longer answer: I wanted to do my own thing. I can't really give you a "good answer," other than to tell you that I had this rebellious need to live my life the way I wanted to live it, not the way God wanted me to live it.

Age 47-present: Love for God and His Word

But God is faithful. He let me drift away from Him, and then He drew me back in a powerful and wonderful way. About 15 years ago He brought me to my knees through a series of relationships and circumstances that still bring tears to my eyes and unspeakable joy to my heart. I am yet another example of a prodigal son who came home to his heavenly Father!

And these past 15 years have been the best years of my life. God and His Word have become so precious to me! I've spent much time reflecting on that foolish decision to walk away from King Jesus. And I've had much regret over those 20 years of spiritual darkness.

Fortunately, Jesus is a God of grace and second chances. He has granted me the gift of repentance and has forgiven all my sins. Amen!

This morning I read Psalm 116. There are some fantastic verses in this psalm that express exactly how I feel about what God has done for me:

"I love the Lord, for he heard my voice; he heard my cry for mercy" (Psalm 116:1).

When I realized the error of my ways, I cried out to God for mercy. And He heard that prayer! Why? Because . . .

"The Lord is gracious and righteous; our God is full of compassion" (Psalm 116:5).

Now I can say with the psalmist: "Be at rest once more, Oh my soul, for the Lord has been good to you" (Psalm 116:7).

When I came back to Jesus, I found myself having an insatiable hunger for the Word of God. I started reading the Bible like never before. I could not put it down! I don't remember having this type of thirst for God's truth, even when I was a seminary student. This was different.

I also found myself not only wanting to study the Word incessantly, but I had a new eagerness to obey God's Word. The psalmist's words became mine:

"I delight in your commands because I love them. I lift up my hands to your commands, which I love, and I meditate on your decrees" (Psalm 119:47-48).

"Oh, how I love your law! I meditate on it all day long" (Psalm 119:97).

"I obey your statutes, for I love them greatly" (Psalm 119:167).

God has done an amazing work in my soul. He did some major heart surgery – taking out my heart of stone and giving me a heart of flesh, just as He promised in Ezekiel 36:25-27. He's given me a passion for His truth as revealed in the written Word, and I am so thankful for that!

God has also given me an intense desire to communicate His truth to people, and writing is one of the best ways I know to do that. So I'm writing this book to help you to see what an incredible resource we have in our hands when we pick up the Bible and read it.

Perhaps you've been reading the Bible for years but have found it difficult lately to spend quality time in the Word. Or perhaps you are a new believer and are just starting out on this journey of following Jesus. Or maybe you're walking close to the Lord, but know that there is room for improvement – you know that your relationship with

Jesus can always grow deeper, and you're looking for ways to pursue even greater intimacy with Him.

Regardless of where you're at right now, this book will show you 10 reasons to read the Bible. There are certainly more than 10 reasons to read the Bible, but these are what I call my "Top Ten" reasons. These are the ones that have become most precious to me over the past few years.

The other thing to note about these reasons is this: each of the reasons also has a corresponding benefit. God wants to bless us when we read His Word. In fact, He has promised to do precisely that.

"Blessed is the one who reads the words of this prophecy, and blessed are those who hear it and take to heart what is written in it, because the time is near" (Revelation 1:3).

I believe that what the Apostle John says here about the book of Revelation is also applicable to the entire Bible. Do you want to be blessed by God? I sure do. Well, here's a surefire way to open the floodgates of heaven on your life – by reading and hearing and taking to heart the Word of God.

Once you start learning these 10 reasons/benefits, I think you'll see why I had a hard time deciding on the title for this book. I picked "Top 10 Reasons to Read the Bible Today: The Life-Changing Benefits of Daily Bible

Reading." But it could also be called "Top 10 Benefits of Reading the Bible Today: The Life-Changing Reasons for Daily Bible Reading."

These "reasons" and "benefits" are intertwined; they are interchangeable. This excites me and gives me even more motivation to tell everyone I can about God and His Word.

In the Evidence Bible, Ray Comfort tells this modern parable:

"A young man once received a letter from a lawyer. The letter said: 'You have been left money by your grandmother.' So he went in to the lawyer, sat in his office, and the lawyer read him the letter. It (the last will and testament of his grandmother) said: 'I hereby leave my grandson $20,000 and my Bible, and all that it contains.' Well, he knew what the Bible contained, so he took that old Bible with its brass clasps and stuck it on the high shelf in his room. Then he spent that $20,000 in about three months, and lived his life as a pauper, barely scraping for every meal and the clothes on his back. About sixty years later his relatives had to come and take him away -- he was so destitute. As he reached up to get a hold of that old Bible off the shelf, and as his trembling hands grabbed it, it suddenly slipped out of his hands and fell on the floor and opened up to reveal a $100 bill between every page! That man could have lived his life in luxury but didn't, simply because of his prejudice."

I wasted 20 years of my life by living like this man. I knew the Bible was full of the treasures of heaven, but chose to ignore it. I am so glad that God saw fit to bring me back, and not a day goes by that I don't hunger and thirst for the pure spiritual milk of the Word. I don't ever want to ignore God's Word!

I've lived my life *without* God and His Word, and I've lived my live *with* God and His Word. For the rest of my days, may God grant me the grace to remain faithful to Him by spending time reading and obeying His Word.

How about you? How would you describe your relationship to God and His Word today? My prayer is that by reading this book, you too will experience the joy of knowing and obeying God by knowing and obeying His Word.

Why You Should Read This Book

There are at least five types of people who should read this book. As you read the following descriptions, please take a look at yourself and see which person you most identify with.

Person #1

You are a Christian but often lack the desire to read the Bible. Most days it's a struggle to open The Book. And so you usually don't. This lack of motivation to spend time in the Word can continue for days, weeks or even months.

You're a very busy person. You have a full-time job (inside and/or outside the home). Perhaps you have children and church activities and errands and a never-ending Things To Do list. It's easy to say, "I just don't have time to read the Bible. I'll get what I need to grow spiritually from the Sunday sermon. Plus I go to Bible study whenever I can." So reading the Bible on your own is not a regular part of your life.

Person #2

You are a Christian, and you've had a love for the Word for some time. Over the years you've have stretches when regular Bible time was a source of much joy. You've read much of the Bible and have done several in-depth Bible studies.

But for some reason, lately that joy in the Word has diminished. You're not sure why, but you haven't been spending as much time in the Word as you used to. Bible reading was once a habit, and now it's not. You know you need to do something about it. You'd like the get that habit back, but you're not quite sure how to make it happen.

Person #3

You are a new Christian. You're just starting out on this journey of following Jesus. You've gotten involved in a local church and have met people who know a lot more about the Bible than you do. You hear your Christian friends talk about reading the Bible and you'd like to experience the joy of spending time with God in His Word. But you're not really sure how to get started.

Person #4

You may or may not be a Christian. You're not really sure. You've had some exposure to Christianity, but have been sitting on the fence. You may have doubts about whether Jesus Christ is the only way to God. And you may not be convinced that the Bible is the Word of God.

But you're open to hearing more about the Christian faith. You'd like to know more about the Bible. You've heard bits and pieces about this book, but don't really know the big picture. You wonder why Christians talk so much about the Bible. What's the big deal about a book written centuries ago? Why should I read it?

Person #5

You are a Christian who reads the Bible regularly, even daily. And it is sweet. "Quiet Time" is your favorite time of the day. Spending time alone with God in the Word and prayer is a top priority for you, because your desire to know Him and to love Him is strong.

But you know that in this life we never "arrive." You understand that spiritual growth is a process that does not end until we get to heaven. So you long for even greater intimacy with Jesus. You want your time in the Word to be even sweeter. And you will do whatever it takes to experience a deeper relationship with God – Father, Son and Spirit.

Reality Check

Which of these five people do you relate to *most of the time*? I realize that you may see aspects of yourself in two or three of these "Persons." But on *most* days, which of these five people best describes you?

The point of this exercise in self-reflection is this: No matter where you're at in your spiritual journey, getting to the next level will necessitate more quality time in the Word.

Let's revisit these five types of people again. And may I offer some words of advice and encouragement, because I do care deeply about you and where you're headed spiritually?

Person #1: If you are rarely read the Bible, please understand how much you are sabotaging your spiritual growth. You're like a world class athlete who rarely eats and then wonders why he/she underperforms in competition.

Person #2: If you've gotten out of the habit of regular Bible reading, you are treading on thin ice. You were climbing Mt. Everest, but now you're on a slippery slope and it could be just a matter of time before you fall.

Person #3: If you're a new Christian, how many wonderful things await you! But you've got to dig into the Word to experience them.

Person #4: If you're on the fence, how much longer can you waffle in indecision? Your eternal destiny depends on finding the truth contained in the Bible. Why not begin today?

Person #5: To the one who is following Jesus closely, I say, "The best is yet to come!" What you are experiencing now can be multiplied further. How awesome is that!"

Wherever you're at, I plead with you to take to heart this reality: Reading the Bible is critical to your spiritual growth.

And this book will show you why that is true.

As you read the "Top 10 Reasons to Read the Bible Today," you'll discover how much God has done to provide everything you need to have a closer relationship with Him.

Peter says it well:

"His divine power has given us everything we need for life and godliness through our knowledge of him who called us by his glory and goodness. Through these he has given us his very great and precious promises, so that through them you may participate in the divine nature and escape the corruption in the world caused by evil desires" (2 Peter 1:3-4).

The power we need to live a godly life is available to us. And we can experience increasing godliness ("the divine nature"). But *how*? Through our *knowledge* of God and through the *promises* of God. And the only source of knowing God and His promises is the written Word of God.

15

I get quite excited just thinking about what God has done for us by providing His Word so we can understand Him and His purposes. Amen?

Of course, if you're content to stay where you're at, then there is no need for you to read this book. But if you want to experience stronger faith, greater joy and deeper peace, then this book is for you. It's as simple as that.

Are you ready to dive in? Let's get started!

Chapter 1:
The Bible Has Authority over Our Lives

I love old TV commercials. Perhaps you remember this vintage 1979 advertisement. Two men are talking about investments over dinner. One of them says, "You'll never regret the purchase of a good stock. My broker says it's a real good buy. What does your broker say?"

The other man replies, "Well, my broker is E.F. Hutton, and E.F. Hutton says . . ."

At this point, everyone in the restaurant "leans in" to hear what the man is about to say – the other diners at every table, all the waiters and busboys, and even the maître d on the other side of the room has his hand up to his ear so he can hear what E.F. Hutton has to say.

We never hear what the E.F. Hutton client says, however, because what happens next is the voiceover of the company spokesperson: "When E.F. Hutton talks, people listen."

You can watch this classic 30-second commercial here:

https://www.youtube.com/watch?v=2_ygqPepLjM

Founded in 1904, E.F. Hutton became one of America's largest brokerage firms of the 20th century, growing to over 19,000 employees in the 1980's. These iconic commercials all ended with the famous slogan, "When E.F. Hutton talks, people listen."

Many of their commercials featured two men having a discussion about their portfolios in a variety of places – in a restaurant, on an airplane, at the health club, or at the airport. It didn't matter where they were or what they were doing, as soon as the words "My broker is E.F. Hutton, and E.F. Hutton says" were spoken, people all around stopped what they were doing and took notice.

Everyone wanted to hear what E.F. Hutton says, because E.F. Hutton was a highly regarded source of valuable and authoritative investment advice.

People benefitted greatly from the words of E.F. Hutton. No doubt thousands of investors made millions of dollars by listening to their stockbrokers at this prestigious company.

Why did people listen to E.F. Hutton? Because E.F. Hutton was the repository of sound financial wisdom. They were an authority in the world of investments.

Likewise, believers have the ultimate source of *spiritual* wisdom at their disposal. The God of the universe has spoken clearly and powerfully in His written Word. The question we must ask ourselves is this: When God talks, do the people of God listen?

How Do We Know That God Speaks?

The first reason we should spend much quality time reading the Bible is because the Bible claims to be the Word of God. Make no mistake, this is one of the main teachings of Scripture. From Genesis to Revelation, phrases like "God says" or "Thus says the Lord" appear over 3,800 times! That is the unequivocal pronouncement of the Bible about the Bible.

Theologians call this teaching "the inspiration of Scripture." Let's take a closer look at one of orthodox Christianity's most treasured doctrines, for this has been the belief of godly men and women for centuries.

The Key Passage

2 Timothy 3:16-17 is the Bible's premiere passage on inspiration. "All Scripture is God-breathed and is useful for teaching, rebuking, correcting and training in righteousness, so that the servant of God may be thoroughly equipped for every good work."

Yet we do not find the word "inspiration" in the NIV's rendering. Hmm.

One of my favorite ways to unpack the meaning of a verse is to compare several translations. Let's take a look at the first part of 2 Timothy 3:16.

NKJV: All Scripture is given by inspiration of God.

NRSV: All scripture is inspired by God.

NASB: All Scripture is inspired by God.

NIV: All Scripture is God-breathed.

ESV: All Scripture is breathed out by God.

The New King James (NKJV), the New Revised Standard (NRSV), and the New American Standard (NASB) all like the word "inspiration" or "inspired." But the NIV and ESV take a different approach, and I'm glad they do, because the concept of Scripture being "breathed out by God" captures the essence of the Greek word Paul uses here. This is the literal meaning of the text.

When we say, "the Bible is inspired by God," what do mean? Wayne Grudem says it succinctly: "All the words in Scripture are God's words" (Systematic Theology). He spoke them. They came from His mouth. He breathed them out.

As John MacArthur explains, "Sometimes God told the Bible writers the exact words to say (e.g., Jer 1:9), but more often He used their minds, vocabularies, and experiences to produce His own perfect infallible, inerrant Word . . . So identified is God with His Word that when Scripture speaks, God speaks" (The MacArthur Study Bible).

Here's another way to say it: ultimately, God wrote the Bible. Yes, human authors were involved in the writing of Scripture. And there is a sense in which the Bible is a human book. God used some 40 men over 1,600 years to record the 66 books of Protestant Bible. And their unique personalities, literary styles and cultural backgrounds are reflected throughout.

But the Bible is first and foremost a divine book. And we believe it is the only book written by the one true God of the universe. "In hundreds of passages, the Bible declares or takes the position explicitly or implicitly that it is nothing less than the very Word of God" (www.Bible.org).

Perhaps this is a different meaning of "inspiration" than you've heard before. Modern usage of the word can put quite a different spin on it. We often say, "That movie really inspired me." By that we mean that I have a new surge of enthusiasm. Webster's Dictionary defines "inspire" as "to influence, motivate or produce a feeling" or "to cause someone to have a feeling or emotion." This contemporary meaning is not what the Bible means by inspiration.

As MacArthur put it: "When Scripture speaks, God speaks." Or, what God says, Scripture says. We find examples of both in the Bible.

What God Says, Scripture Says

In Genesis 12:1-3 we read the words that God spoke to Abraham: "The Lord had said to Abraham, 'Leave your country, your people and your father's household and go to the land I will show you.'" This is followed by several famous promises known as the Abrahamic Covenant, which concludes with God saying, "All peoples on earth will be blessed through you."

In Galatians 3:8, however, when Paul quotes Genesis 12:3, he writes, "The Scripture foresaw that God would justify the Gentiles by faith, and announced the gospel in advance to Abraham: 'All nations will be blessed through you.'"

This is subtle yet most significant. Paul does not say that *God* spoke in Genesis 12:3. Instead, He is saying that the *Scripture* "announced" something in Genesis 12:3. God speaking and Scripture speaking are interchangeable.

You can find a similar situation when comparing Exodus 9:16, where God is speaking to Pharaoh, and Romans 9:17, which indicates that "the Scripture says to Pharaoh, 'I raised you up for this very purpose, that I might display my power in you and that my name might be proclaimed in all the earth.'"

What Scripture Says, God Says

Here's one more example that warrants our consideration because Jesus Himself affirmed the interchangeability of Scripture and God. In Matthew 19:4-5, Jesus quotes God as saying, "For this reason a man will leave his father and mother and be united to his wife, and the two will become one flesh." Jesus is referencing Genesis 2:24. But God is not speaking in Genesis 2:24! Moses wrote that verse without any mention of God speaking. Now we affirm: What Scripture says, God says.

As you reflect on these great truths of biblical Christianity, I trust you are filled with much thanksgiving and praise to our great God and Savior! He has revealed Himself and His Son through the pages of Holy Scripture. What a mind-blowing gift we have!

God has spoken, and now it's up to us to listen.

Please consider this simple yet powerful concept: The inspiration of Scripture leads logically to the infallibility and inerrancy of Scripture.

We can express this by the following statements:

1. Scripture is the very Word of God. 2 Timothy 3:16 makes this clear. "All Scripture is God-breathed."

2. God cannot lie. He always speaks the truth. Hebrews 6:18, "It is impossible for God to lie."

3. Therefore the Scriptures contain no errors. Psalm 12:6, "And the words of the Lord are flawless, like silver refined in a furnace of clay, purified seven times."

Psalm 18:30, "As for God, his way is perfect; the word of the Lord is flawless."

Psalm 119:60, "All your words are true."

Wow! Isn't this wonderful news? With so much uncertainty in the world, aren't we blessed to have the perfect Word of God in our hands to read and treasure every day of our lives?

How are you feeling today about the inspiration and infallibility of the Bible? Do you have gratitude in your heart toward God for the amazing gift of Scripture? Can you say with the Psalmist, "At midnight I rise to give thanks for your righteous laws" (Psalm 119:62).

Do you ever wake up in the middle of the night? I do. Today I woke up at 3:00 am. I'm not sure why. And it doesn't really matter. But I was wide awake and ready to go! I started working on this book yesterday and completed the outline. So my mind is filled with thoughts of God's Word and how I'd like to communicate these truths to you.

When I woke up, I thought, "Oh boy. Shouldn't I go back to bed and get some more sleep?" But I was too excited about writing. I wanted to sit down and pour myself into the study of the greatest Book ever written – the Bible!

Do you ever have moments like that? You get so excited about what God is teaching you, you can't even sleep! Now don't misunderstand me. I usually sleep like a log. But every now and then, I do wake up a few hours early, and when that happens, I head right for my Bible and read it or study it or write about it.

I do have times when my heart soars with delight in the Word and I can honestly say to God, "How sweet are your words to my taste, sweeter than honey to my mouth" (Psalm 119:103).

But passion for the Word isn't enough. God expects more from us than that. Let's reflect on another sequence of logical statements:

1. God is the King of the universe and therefore has authority over my life.

"The Lord reigns forever." (Psalm 9:7)

"The Lord is king forever and ever." (Psalm 10:16)

2. Ultimately, God wrote the Bible.

"All Scripture is God-breathed." (2 Timothy 3:16)

3. Therefore, the Bible has authority over my life.

"All Scripture is God-breathed and is useful for teaching, rebuking, correcting and training in righteousness, so that the servant of God may be thoroughly equipped for every good work." (2 Timothy 3:16-17)

The Bible was written to teach us, rebuke us, correct us, and train us in righteousness. And we'll be talking more about the role of Scripture in our sanctification, the never-ending process of becoming pure and more Christ-like.

Right now, I'd like us to focus on this question: If God and the Scriptures have authority over our lives, what should be our response? In a word, submission. Loving obedience from the heart is the only appropriate response.

We read the Bible for many reasons. The first one is this: We read the Bible because it is the authoritative Word of God and therefore we have an intense desire to know it so we can obey it.

But this obedience is not to be confused with mere external adherence to a set of rules. The Bible is not a To Do List. Rather, because God has done so much for us, we love Him. "We love because he first loved us" (1 John 4:19). And the outpouring of that love is expressed in a life of heartfelt obedience to His Word. Jesus said,

"If you love me, you will obey what I command" (John 14:15).

We want to do His will by obeying His Word, so we devote much time and energy to knowing and understanding His will as revealed in His Word. Then the psalmist's prayer can become ours:

"Give me understanding, so that I can keep your law and obey it with all my heart." (Psalm 119:34)

"I obey your statutes, for I love them greatly." (Psalm 119:167)

May it be so!

SUMMARY:

Reason #1: We read the Bible because it is the inspired Word of God and therefore has authority over our lives.

Benefit: countless blessings and rewards of living in obedience to the will of God.

Key Passages:
2 Timothy 3:16-17
Psalm 12:6
Psalm 18:30
Psalm 116:60

Chapter 2:
The Bible Teaches God's Way of Salvation

The second reason we read the Bible takes us to one of the most glorious truths of the Christian faith.

But before diving into Reason/Benefit #2, however, can I ask you a personal question?

Do you know what your name means?

Go ahead and "google" your first name right now and see if you can discover the meaning of your name. I haven't done this for myself in a while, so I'll do it, too. Then we'll come back together in a few minutes. Go online and type in "meaning of YourFirstName." For me, that will look like this: "meaning of Wayne." (The quotation marks are optional.)

Ready? Go for it!

(Let's pause while we search the internet.)

I'm done. How about you? How did it go? Did find out the meaning of your name?

I did. I found a couple interesting hits.

http://www.sheknows.com/baby-names/name/wayne

American Meaning: The name Wayne is an American baby name. In American the meaning of the name Wayne is: Craftsman; wagon-wright; wagon driver. Famous Bearer: U.S. Actor John Wayne.

http://www.behindthename.com/name/wayne

"From an occupational surname meaning "wagon maker," derived from Old English "wagon."

So I'm a wagon maker!

I know for a fact that my becoming a wagon maker was the furthest thing from my parents' mind when they named me. I was born in 1957. John Wayne was a popular actor then, so my parents gave me this name because they liked him.

People rarely give names these days because of the meaning of the name. We pick a name because it sounds nice or because someone else in the family has that name. Or we name our child after someone famous ☺

In Bible times that wasn't the case. 2000 years ago names had great significance, and names were picked because of the meaning behind the word.

The Bible says there is a name that is above every name. "Therefore God exalted him to the highest place and gave him a name that is above every name, that at the name of Jesus every knee should bow, in heaven and on earth and under the earth, and every tongue confess that Jesus is Lord, to the glory of God the Father" (Philippians 2:9-11).

Do you know the meaning of the name "Jesus"? The Bible tells us. In Matthew 1:21, the angel said to Joseph, "You are to give him the name Jesus, because he will save his people from their sins." The name Jesus means "The Lord saves" or simply "Savior."

Jesus' name communicates the purpose of His incarnation. He came to save us. Is this not the clear teaching of Scripture?

John writes, "The Father sent the Son to be the Savior of the world" (1 John 4:14)

Paul writes, "Here is a trustworthy saying that deserves full acceptance: Christ Jesus came into the world to save sinners." (1 Timothy 1:15)

And Jesus Himself said, "The Son of Man came to seek and to save the lost." (Luke 19:10)

The second reason why we love to read the Bible is because it is the only book in which God has revealed the message of salvation from sin through His Son the Lord Jesus Christ.

There are so many passages in the Bible that explain salvation. Paul acknowledges this fact when writing to Timothy. We just looked at 2 Timothy 3:16-17 in the previous chapter when discussing the inspiration of Scripture. And it just so happens that one of the Bible's clearest verses about Scripture as source of the salvation message is 2 Timothy 3:15.

"From infancy you have known the Holy Scriptures, which are able to make you wise for salvation through faith in Christ Jesus." The Bible gives us the wisdom we need to understand, receive and apply God's message of salvation, the gospel of Jesus.

The word "salvation" is a rich word, filled with meaning and significance. It simply means deliverance or rescue, and can be used of both physical salvation (such as being healed of an illness) and spiritual salvation (being saved from sin and all its devastating consequences, including the wrath of God poured out on Judgment Day and eternal punishment in hell).

My favorite way to explain salvation is to use a threefold outline that sees salvation as a past event, a present experience, and a future hope. This approach assumes that you are a Christian and you are looking at your salvation from the perspective of time: past, present and future.

1. Salvation is a past event known as "justification."

The Bible says you have already been saved. It's a done deal. It happened on the day God granted you faith and repentance. Some Christians can remember the exact day and time. Other believers do not know the specific date, and that's OK, too.

The point is this: We *have been saved* from the *penalty* of sin. God has rescued us from His wrath. He has delivered us from hell. Praise God for that! Because the Father poured out His wrath on the Son, His justice has been satisfied and His anger has been spent – on Jesus, who died in our place and took upon Himself the punishment we deserve.

The Bible describes our salvation from sin with the word "justification," a legal term that comes right from the courtroom. It means to "declare righteous." God the Judge pronounces the sinner righteous because the righteousness of Christ has been credited to his account.

Many passages teach that salvation is a past event. Note the tense of each verb in the following verses.

"Therefore, since we *have been justified* through faith, we have peace with God through our Lord Jesus Christ." (Romans 5:1)

"For it is by grace you *have been saved*, through faith." (Ephesians 2:8)

"But when the kindness and love of God our Savior appeared, *he saved us*." (Titus 3:4)

2. Salvation is a present experience known as "sanctification."

The Bible also says that we *are being saved* (every day) from the *power* of sin. Even though God has forgiven our sins and wiped the slate clean through justification, we still have a sin nature and must fight a daily battle against the evil within.

From the day we are born again to the day we die, we need God to save us from the power of sin – everything from lust, anger and greed to lying, stealing and fornication. Temptation will continue to rear its ugly head at us, and the goal of Christian living is to live a life of increasing Christ-likeness and decreasing impurity. This is called "sanctification," another word packed with meaning.

"Sanctification" simply means "holiness." It means to be unique, to be set apart -- from sin and unto God. Of course, only God is perfectly sanctified and holy. But we are to obtain a measure of his holiness through the lifelong journey of sanctification. God tells us, in no uncertain terms, to "Be holy, because I am holy" (1 Peter 1:16). "Just as he who called you is holy, so be holy in all you do" (1 Peter 1:15).

Note the following passages that teach salvation is a present experience that occurs daily.

"By one sacrifice he has made perfect forever those who *are being made holy*." (Hebrews 10:14). Note that this verse mentions both justification (God has made us perfect by declaring us righteous in His sight because of Jesus) and sanctification (we are being made holy by becoming more and more like Jesus).

"By this gospel you *are being saved*, if you hold firmly to the word I preached to you." (1 Corinthians 15:2)

"For we are to God the aroma of Christ among those who *are being saved* and those who are perishing." (2 Corinthians 2:15)

3. Salvation is a future hope known as "glorification."

One day we will die and be transported immediately into the presence of Christ. "To be away from the body and at home with the Lord" (2 Corinthians 5:8). Oh what a wonderful day that will be!

This is our hope – to spend eternity with King Jesus. Paul describes the incredible glory of heaven in one of the Bible's most precious passages:

"And we know that in all things God works for the good of those who love him, who have been called according to his purpose. For those God foreknew he also predestined to be conformed to the image of his Son, that he might be the firstborn among many brothers and sisters. And those he predestined, he also called; those he called, he also justified; those he justified, he also glorified." (Romans 8:28-30)

Interestingly, Paul uses the past tense to describe our future hope of glorification. "Those he justified, he also glorified." Because our inheritance in heaven is based on the promises of God, we can speak of it as if it has already happened!

Other passages use the future tense to describe the final phase of our salvation:

"Since we have now been justified by his blood, how much more *shall we be saved* from God's wrath through him!" (Romans 5:9)

"We believe that *we will be saved* through the grace of the Lord Jesus Christ." (Acts 15:11).

To summarize . . .

Salvation is a past event. "God saved me." I have been saved from the penalty of sin. That's justification.

Salvation is a present experience. "God is saving me." I am being saved from the power of sin. That's sanctification.

Salvation is a future hope. "God will save me." I will be saved from the presence of sin. That's glorification.

And how do we know all this? Because God has revealed the gospel of salvation in His Word. Without the Scriptures, we would be clueless regarding our lost condition and God's remedy for it.

We must read and study the Bible so we can know, understand and apply the message of God's grace in Christ Jesus.

Think about this: What would the world be like today if there was no Bible? Fortunately, God has not left us in the dark about our sinful condition and His solution to our #1 problem. Not only did He send Jesus to provide salvation from sin, He then miraculously guided His closest followers to record the life, death, resurrection and teachings of Jesus in the four gospels of Matthew, Mark, Luke and John.

After Jesus ascended to heaven and the early church began to grow, God then directed Luke to write the book of Acts, so we would know how the message of salvation was proclaimed in "Jerusalem, and in all Judea and Samaria, and to the ends of the earth" (Acts 1:8).

During these formative years of the church's existence, God also led Paul, John, Peter, James and Jude to write letters to the new Christian communities springing up throughout the Roman Empire. God saw fit to preserve some of these "epistles" so that by the end of the first century, there were 27 "books" (4 gospels + Acts + 22 letters) that became our New Testament.

Oh, may we never take the Word of God for granted! Many have died for this book. When you pick up your Bible, you are holding the world's most precious possession in your hand – the inspired, infallible, authoritative Word of God.

This is no ordinary book. It contains the words of eternal life. Without it, we are lost forever. By reading this book, God can teach us how to find salvation from the penalty, power and presence of sin through His Son Jesus Christ.

SUMMARY

Reason #2: We read the Bible because it teaches us God's way of salvation. The name "Jesus" means Savior.

Benefit: in this life, we can be saved from the penalty and power of sin; in the next life, we spend eternity in heaven instead of hell. Salvation from sin and all its consequences in both this life and the next.

Key Passages:
2 Timothy 3:15
Ephesians 2:8
Hebrews 2:14
Romans 5:9

Chapter 3:
The Bible Strengthens Our Faith

In Mark 9:14-32 we read a fascinating account of Jesus' healing of a demon-possessed boy. The boy's father brought his son to the disciples while Jesus was on a mountain with Peter, James and John, where He revealed His glory and had a conversation with Moses and Elijah (Mark 9:1-13).

Meanwhile the disciples were unable to heal the boy. When Jesus arrives on the scene, the man tells Him, "I asked your disciples to drive out the spirit, but they could not" (v. 18).

Jesus then expresses his frustration with His followers. "O unbelieving generation, how long shall I stay with you? How long will I put up with you? Bring the boy to me" (v. 19).

"So they brought him. When the spirit saw Jesus, it immediately threw the boy into a convulsion. He fell to the ground and rolled around, foaming at the mouth.

"Jesus asked the boy's father, 'How long has he been like this?'"

'From childhood,' he answered. 'It has often thrown him into fire or water to kill him. But if you can do anything, take pity on us and help us.'

'If you can?' said Jesus. 'Everything is possible for him who believes.'

"Immediately the boy's father exclaimed, 'I do believe; help me overcome my unbelief.'

"When Jesus saw that a crowd was running to the scene, he rebuked the evil spirit. 'You deaf and dumb spirit, I command you, come out of him and never enter him again.'

"The spirit shrieked, convulsed him violently and came out. The boy looked so much like a corpse that many said, 'He's dead.' But Jesus took him by the hand and lifted him to his feet, and he stood up" (v. 20-27).

Like every story in the gospels, Jesus is the hero. He is the focus. What an amazing display of the power of Jesus!

The glory of Jesus stands in stark contrast to the floundering disciples. Our Lord describes them as "unbelieving" (v. 19).

The boy's father is also a key player in this account. He has expressed his desire for Jesus to heal his son. "But if you can do anything, take pity on us and help us" (v. 23).

Jesus' response seems a bit sarcastic. "*If* you can?" Hmm. Jesus is questioning the man's faith. It's as if Jesus is saying, "You brought your son to me to be healed. But I'm not sure you really believe I can do this."

The man's next comment reveals that Jesus read his heart like a book. "I do believe; help me overcome my unbelief!" (v. 24).

I love Mark 9:24. This man's honest confession of faith and doubt in the same breath is a beautiful thing.

Can you identify with this man? I can.

Do you believe, yet struggle with unbelief? I do. Every day.

I'm so glad God included this story in the Bible. It is so encouraging to encounter a man who speaks on behalf of every believer.

We believe. That's why we're called believers!

Yet we have times when doubt overcomes us and we find ourselves swimming in a sea of uncertainty.

Fortunately, God comes to our rescue and provides the remedy for our tendency to waver. Do you want a stronger faith? I'm sure you do – that's why you're reading this book. I do. My desire for a growing faith burns in my heart. What can we do to make it happen?

Fortunately, the Word of God tells us how to acquire more faith.

This is another fantastic benefit of reading and studying the Bible. When we immerse ourselves in Scripture, God gives us stronger faith.

Let's unpack this vital truth.

1. Faith is a gift from God to us.

Philippians 1:29 tells us that, "It has been granted to you on behalf of Christ not only to believe on him, but also to suffer for him." Believing on Jesus is something we first did because God **granted** us the ability to believe. Faith is not something we create with our own power; it is something that God gives to us. We can only believe because we receive faith from Him.

Ephesians 2:8 teaches the same truth. "For it is by grace you have been saved, through faith – and this not from yourselves, **it is the gift of God.**" What is the gift of God? Grace, salvation and faith are all gifts from His hand.

Here's another verse that I find most encouraging. "What do you have that you did not receive?" (1 Corinthians 4:7). Answer: Nothing! Everything we have comes to us from the gracious hand of God. If you have faith, how did you get it? As a gift. You received it from the Creator of the universe.

2. Since God is the source of faith, we must go to Him and ask Him to increase our faith.

The father's plea to Jesus in Mark 9:24 is a model prayer for us. "I do believe; help me overcome my unbelief!" Do you want more faith? Then ask God for it. Could it be that we lack faith simply because we forget to go to God in prayer and ask for it? James 4:2 reminds us, "You do not have, because you do not ask God."

3. God bestows faith on us when we listen to His Word.

Romans 10:17 teaches this so clearly. "Consequently, faith comes from hearing the message, and the message is heard through the word of Christ."

Think back to your conversion. As you reflect on all the conversations, events and circumstances that preceded your coming to Christ for salvation, somewhere along the line you heard the gospel, right? That's how God saves people. The "word of Christ" was communicated to you in any number of ways. You heard a sermon or read a book or went to a Bible study or had a discussion with a friend. You heard "the message," the Word of God.

And while you were listening, God opened the eyes of your heart, supernaturally softening your heart of stone and giving you a heart of flesh. He gave you understanding of your true condition before a holy God;

your sin became "utterly sinful" (Romans 7:13). He enabled you to see how Jesus' death and resurrection are the answer to your sin problem. *And God gave you faith in Christ because you were listening to His Word.*

Now that you are a believer, this is how God continues to work in your life. He increases your faith when you expose yourself to His truth as revealed in the Scriptures.

4. Therefore, to strengthen your faith, spend more time in the Word.

This is not rocket science. It really is that simple. The more time you devote to the hearing of God's Word, the more your faith will grow and the stronger you'll become.

There are so many wonderful ways to hear the Word. I love the illustration developed by the Navigators – "Getting a grip on God's Word." Our hand is used as an object lesson to remind us of five great ways to spend time in the Word.

https://www.navigators.org/resource/the-word-hand/

1.Hear the Word.

Romans 10:17

This is a reference to the literally meaning of "hear." We listen to a sermon or attend a Bible class. We put ourselves in a position of humble teachability.

2. Read the Word.

Revelation 1:3

Hearing a good Bible-based sermon on Sunday morning is tremendous! But it's not enough. For many professing believers, one weekly 30-minute dose of the Word is all they get. Imagine what your life would be like if you limited yourself to one meal per week? You'd get weak in a hurry, because it is so true that "Seven days without food makes one weak."

We must spend time reading the Word regularly, even daily, or we will not grow and our faith will wither and die.

3. Study the Word.

Acts 17:11

Reading must be enhanced with more in-depth study of the Word. There are so many good resources available to help us dig deeper into God's truth. If you're not sure where to go get Bible study resources, reach out to your Pastor or other mature Christian friend to get some recommendations.

For many Christians, joining a weekly Bible study group is the best way to insure you get solid Bible time.

4. Memorize the Word.

Psalm 19:9-11

This is perhaps the most overlooked method of hearing the Word, especially for adult believers. We seem to think that Scripture memory is only for children. Nothing could be further from the truth!

What did Jesus do when tempted by the devil? He resisted the devil by quoting Scripture from memory. (See Matthew 4:1-11). End result: "Then the devil left him" (Matthew 4:11).

If Jesus memorized Bible verses, how can we not follow in His footsteps?

5. Meditate on the Word.

Psalm 1:2-3

When reading and studying the Word, you'll want to spend time simply thinking about what you're learning, mulling it over and mentally chewing on it. One way to do this is by praying about what you are learning. As you read and study, talk to your heavenly Father as He reveals His truth to you. Focus on the specific ways God wants you to submit to His Word through new attitudes and loving obedience from the heart.

One way to do this is to ask questions of the text, such as:

What does this passage teach me about God?

Is there a sin for me to confess or avoid?

Is there a promise for me to believe?

Is there an good example to imitate or a bad example to avoid?

Is there a command for me to obey?

SUMMARY

Reason #3: We read the Bible because it strengthens and increases our faith. God promises to give us more faith when we spend much quality time in the Word. Our initial belief unto salvation was the result of hearing the Word, and this pattern continues throughout the rest of our lives.

The Benefit: The contentment of living a God-pleasing life, because "without faith, it is impossible to please God" (Hebrews 11:6).

Key Passages:
Philippians 1:29
Ephesians 2:8

1 Corinthians 4:7
Mark 9:24
James 4:2
Romans 10:17

Chapter 4:
The Bible Gives Us A
Changing Life

When we think of the many words used in Scripture to describe the Christian life, what comes to mind? Here's a few to jumpstart this brainstorming session. Saved. Forgiven. Redeemed. Reconciled. Beloved.

On and on we could go. Amen?

How about this one – Changed. On the day God rescued you from the dominion of darkness and brought you into the kingdom of the Son he loves (per Colossians 1:13), you've been on a breathtaking collision course with change, a journey of continuous transformation.

On the day God lifted you out of the slimy pit (per Psalm 40:2), in the twinkling of an eye He changed you from a guilty sinner, with God's death sentence of hell hanging over your head, to a justified saint now clothed in the righteousness of Christ. Could there be a more radical change than that?

And on the day God takes you home, you'll be changed again when death is swallowed up by life everlasting and "we shall be like him, for we shall see him as he is" (1

John 3:2). This change will be radical beyond human comprehension!

In the meantime, we are being changed every day, as God works in us, for us and through us to conform us to the likeness of Christ. There are days when it may not seem like much is happening in this process of sanctification, but rest assured, God is doing what only He can do – He's changing you, one painful yet joy-filled step at a time.

We have been changed. We are being changed. And one day we will be changed forever.

We live "A Constantly Changing Life."

How do we know this to be true? Well, the Bible is crystal clear regarding the effects of saving faith in a true believer. The longer you walk on the path of discipleship, the more aware you'll be of these changes. You'll continue to embrace new attitudes and behaviors while discarding our old sinful habits and thought patters. Make no mistake, the results of your conversion can be summarized in one word: Change.

The Apostle Paul visits the topic of "A Constantly Changing Life" repeatedly in his teachings. Let's take a look at three key passages that demonstrate this.

Passage #1 - Romans 12:1-2
"Do not be conformed any longer to the pattern of this

world, but be transformed by the renewing of your mind. Then you will be able to test and approve what God's will is – his good, pleasing and perfect will."

The command is clear: Be transformed. Paul uses the Greek word from which we get "metamorphosis." We could translate this phrase, "Be changed."

The word only appears four times in the New Testament. In Matthew 17:2 and Mark 9:2 it is rendered "transfigured." "Jesus took Peter, James and John with him and led them up a high mountain, where they were all alone. There he was *transfigured* before them. His clothes became dazzling white, whiter than anyone in the world could bleach them" (Mark 9:2-3).

Jesus changed right before the apostles' eyes, manifesting the glory He had from eternity past but temporarily set aside while taking on human flesh. In heaven we too will shine like the sun!

Until then, how are we to demonstrate our transformation? John MacArthur answers this question quite well. "Just as Christ briefly and in a limited way displayed outwardly his inner, divine nature and glory at the Transfiguration, Christians should outwardly manifest their inner, redeemed natures, not once, however, but daily." (MacArthur Study Bible)

This type of transformation is truly "an inside job," as Paul indicates in the phrase, "by the renewing of your mind." Here we have another word, *renewing*, which is a synonym for change. The Enhanced Strong's Lexicon defines it as "a renewal, renovation, complete change for the better."

How do we *renovate* our minds? By immersing ourselves in the Word of God. "That kind of transformation can occur only as the Holy Spirit changes our thinking through consistent study and meditation of Scripture. The renewed mind is one saturated with and controlled by the word of God" (MacArthur Study Bible).

When I think of a "metamorphosis" in nature, the incredible change that occurs in the life cycle of the butterfly comes to mind. Truly this captures the essence of the change that God works in us. We begin in a cocoon, symbolic of the ugliness of sin and all its putrid consequences in both this life and the next.

Then, one day, God does a miracle by giving us a new heart and a new life. We instantly change into a spiritual butterfly. Even though we'll spend the rest of our life fighting off the remnants of the old life in the cocoon, we have the God-given potential to show a dazzling array of colors when we submit to God's will as revealed in His Word, empowered by the Holy Spirit to fly for His glory.

Passage #2 - Acts 20:32

"Now I commit you to God and to the word of his grace, which can build you up and give you an inheritance among all those who are sanctified."

In our second passage on "A Constantly Changing Life" we move from the analogy of the butterfly to the image of a building project. The phrase "build up" literally means "to build a house, erect a building" (Enhanced Strong's Lexicon). When used figuratively, it means to edify or to strengthen. The point is clear: God wants us to become spiritually stronger and stronger. As the Master Builder, God wants to build us up into a mature man or woman of God.

And how does God do that? What is the means by which God accomplishes this noble goal? "I commit you to God *and to the word of his grace.*" It is God's Word that is the key to our growth from a spiritual hut to a tower of strength. It is the Bible that "can build you up."

Isn't this a wonderful picture of the Christian life? Paul uses the imagery of the building repeatedly to communicate the essence of A Changing Life. Consider these parallel passages:

"So then, just as you received Christ Jesus as Lord, continue to live your lives in him, rooted and **built up in him**, strengthened in the faith as you were taught, and overflowing with thankfulness." (Colossians 2:6-7)

"Consequently, you are no longer foreigners and strangers, but fellow citizens with God's people and also members of his household, **built** on the foundation of the apostles and prophets, with Christ Jesus himself as the chief cornerstone. In him the **whole building** is joined together and rises to become a holy **temple** in the Lord. And in him you too are **being built together** to become a **dwelling** in which God lives by his Spirit. (Ephesians 2:19-22)

Passage #3 – 1 Peter 2:2-3
"Like newborn babies, crave pure spiritual milk, so that by it you may grow up in your salvation, now that you have tasted that the Lord is good."

Our third passage employs yet another insightful analogy. "A Constantly Changing Life" is like the metamorphosis of the butterfly, the building of a house, and according to Peter, the craving of a baby for milk.

Who hasn't heard the scream of a hungry baby? When an infant needs milk, the whole world knows. Note the word Peter used here: crave (NIV). The ESV renders it "long for"; the NKJV, "desire."

Think about your own life. Had any cravings lately? Got any longings or desires? Are you kidding me? By nature, we are factories of desire. We live our lives motivated by longings.

Whether it's the craving for a particular food during pregnancy or the longing of a lost child at the mall, desires are everywhere. Alcoholic and Chocoholic are both household words.

God wants us to crave "pure spiritual milk" (NIV), an obvious reference to the Word of God. The NASB communicates this much more clearly – "long for the pure milk *of the word.*"

And why should the Word be the object of our deepest desires? "So that by it you may grow up in your salvation." The analogy is self-evident. A baby will die without milk. And you will die without the Word.

A baby can grow physically only when fed regularly. And you can grow spiritually only when fed regularly.

The word-pictures of Scripture are divinely appointed to teach truth powerfully. If a baby doesn't get milk, he'll become weak and susceptible to illness, disease and even death. An undernourished or malnourished baby is a tragic thing.

Likewise, a believer who doesn't nourish himself on the Word will become weak and susceptible to all manner of spiritual illness, disease, and even death.

An undernourished or malnourished believer will have a faith that wavers at the slightest trial. He will succumb to the temptations of the world, the flesh and the devil, and wonder, "Why can't I say no to sin and yes to God?"

Reality check: How is your desire for the Word? Do you long for the Word like a baby longs for milk? Do you crave time in the written Word because you crave time with Jesus the Living Word?

If your desire for the Word seems lethargic lately, here's how to cultivate it. Note how Peter ends verse 3: "now that you have tasted that the Lord is good."

To stimulate your hunger for the Word, spend time "tasting" the goodness of God by reading, studying and meditating on a passage like Ephesians 1:3-14. Here Paul unpacks the many "spiritual blessings" we have "in Christ."

In just twelve verses Paul mentions many precious truths about salvation: election, justification, adoption, predestination, grace, redemption, forgiveness, hope, inheritance, and the sealing of the Holy Spirit.

I urge you to spend time unpacking the meaning of each of these words. There is a treasure chest of spiritual gems in this passage. Open it up and feast your eyes on the beauty of Christ and all He has done for us on the cross!

Then, you will "taste and see that the Lord is good" (Psalm 34:8). And the result will be this: You will grow like a well-fed baby. God will build you up into a building that only He can create. And you will be transformed like a butterfly.

You will be changed! And God will do it by the word of his grace, the pure milk of the Word.

SUMMARY

Reason #4: We read the Bible because it leads us on the path of increasing godliness – "The Constantly Changing Life."

Benefit: As we grow spiritually, by the grace and power of God we become stronger and better able to handle whatever happens in life.

Key Passages:
Romans 12:1-2
Acts 20:32
1 Peter 2:3-4

Chapter 5:
The Bible Provides Power to Kill Our Sin

How would you complete this sentence: Christianity is the most _____ religion in the world. Take a moment to fill in the blank. I'll wait right here.

How did you respond?

How about this: Christianity is the most *loving* religion in the world. Would you agree? Or what about this one: Christianity is the most *truthful* religion in the world?

What other word would you use to describe Christianity? Kind. Compassionate. Helpful. Perhaps many words like that come to mind.

Here's one that might surprise you: Christianity is the most *violent* religion in the world.

If you are a Christian, did you know that are commanded by Jesus Christ Himself to perform gruesome acts of violence?

"If your hand causes you to sin, cut it off. It is better for you to enter life maimed than with two hands to go into hell, where the fire never goes out" (Mark 9:43). Jesus said that. And He didn't stop there.

"If your foot causes you to sin, cut it off. It is better for you to enter life crippled than to have two feet and be thrown into hell" (Mark 9:45).

And if that wasn't enough gore, He then said, "If your eye causes you to sin, pluck it out. It is better for you to enter the kingdom of God with one eye than to have two eyes and be thrown into hell, where their worm does not die, and the fire is not quenched" (Mark 9:47-48).

"But Jesus was speaking figuratively," you say. Of course He was. But that only makes the meaning more severe. We only use figurative language when ordinary language doesn't do the job. Jesus is saying that we must do whatever it takes to remove sin from our lives.

Or how about this verse, written by the Apostle Paul: "If you live according to the sinful nature, you will die; but if by the Spirit you *put to death* the misdeeds of the body, you will live" (Romans 8:13).

We are commanded to perform gruesome acts of violence, including killing and murder – not against people, but against ourselves. What are we to kill? "The misdeeds of the body." And what are these "misdeeds"? Our sins. We are commanded by God to take drastic measures against our sin, and to get rid of it by killing it.

I rest my case: Christianity is the most violent religion in the world.

In a previous chapter we discussed the meaning of salvation. A true Christian is a person who has received the gift of salvation through faith in Jesus Christ. Salvation from what? "You are to give him the name Jesus, because He will save his people from their *sins*" (Matthew 1:21).

Salvation means to be rescued from our sins. *Justification* is the one-time past event that through which God provides salvation from the penalty of sin. *Sanctification* is the ongoing present experience in which God provides salvation from the power of sin. And *glorification* is the future hope of God providing salvation from the presence of sin.

In this chapter I'd like to focus on *sanctification*. This is such a crucial part of our salvation. It's one of the keys to knowing whether or not you are truly a Christian, for salvation is a "package deal." If you receive salvation, you get all three components. No one receives justification only, or sanctification only, or glorification only.

Here's another way to say it: If I claim to be justified, then I better be getting sanctified. Or, if I am not being saved from the power of my sin, then I was never saved from the penalty of my sin. And if I was never saved from the penalty of sin, then I'm on the way to hell, no matter what I say or how many times I've prayed the sinner's prayer or walked down the aisle or raised my hand or been baptized.

Sanctification (holiness) is the evidence that my profession of faith is genuine and that I am truly saved.

"Without holiness no one will see the Lord" (Hebrews 12:14). The word "holiness" can also be translated "sanctification."

The Apostle John had much to say about the evidence of true conversion, especially in his first letter.

"We know that we have come to know him if we obey his commands. The man who says, 'I know him,' but does not do what he commands is a liar, and the truth is not in him" (1 John 2:3-4).

Back to Paul and Romans 8:13. The last half of the verse says, "if by the Spirit you put to death the misdeeds of the body, you will live." I take that to mean this: If you are being sanctified, you will live forever in heaven. If you are being saved from the power of sin, you have eternal life.

Let's unpack the first half of the verse. "If you live according to the sinful nature, you will die." I take that to mean that if you are not being sanctified, you'll end up in the lake of fire.

OK. Time out. Let's take a break and let the weight of these truths rest upon us. This is heavy stuff! This is eternity we're talking about. Life and death. Eternal life and eternal death.

I realize I may be discussing the Bible in a way you've not heard before. Perhaps you've come from an evangelical background that tends to emphasize the benefits of salvation while ignoring the demands of discipleship. I'm all for talking about the countless blessings of God's grace and mercy in Christ! But there's more to the gospel than going to heaven and living happily after. Much more.

Please do not misunderstand me. I'm not teaching salvation by works. I believe in salvation by grace alone, through faith alone, in Christ alone. "The gift of God is eternal life in Christ Jesus our Lord" (Romans 6:23). "For it is by grace you have been saved, through faith – and this not from yourselves, it is the gift of God – not by works, so that no one can boast" (Ephesians 2:8-10).

Yes, salvation is free. But it will cost you everything. This is one of the great paradoxes of Scripture. When we talk about sanctification, we're talking about the cost of discipleship. The gospel is not so much an invitation as it is a command. Jesus proclaimed, "The time has come. The kingdom of God is near. Repent and believe the good news!" (Mark 1:15). Jesus also said, "If anyone would come after me, he must deny himself and take up his cross daily and follow me. For whoever wants to save his life will lose it, but whoever loses his life for me will save it" (Luke 9:23-24).

It can be difficult to find the right balance in our teaching between the blessings and demands of salvation. But we must address both because the Bible addresses both. The passages we discussed above (Mark 9:43-48, Romans 8:13, Hebrews 12:14) can be a hard pill to swallow for some believers. I trust you'll see I have your best interests at heart when I say something radical like "Christianity is the most violent religion in the world."

When I read the Bible, I ask questions. Here's a good one to start with: Why did Jesus say "cut it off" and "pluck it out"? Why did Paul say "put to death"? I can think of several possible answers to this question. The first thing that comes to mind is that Jesus and Paul were addressing those who promote "cheap grace" and "easy believism" – the mistaken notion that we can simply "believe" (or *profess* to believe) and then live however we want, turning God's mercy into a license to sin. Or as John put it – we must be careful not to merely *claim* to know Jesus but then disregard His instructions for living a holy life with a heartfelt obedience to His commands.

Here's another question to ask: "How do I kill sin? How do I put to death the misdeeds of my body?"

Fortunately, God tells us how to kill sin . . . in the Bible. This is our next reason/benefit for reading the Bible. It tells us exactly how to kill sin and live a holy life. It's no mystery. It's right here in the pages of Scripture.

The night before he was crucified, Jesus prayed an amazing prayer, and it's recorded in John 17. Jesus loves me, this I know, for the Bible tells me so. You want to know how much Jesus loves you? Read John 17. Oh how He loves us in this prayer.

Listen to what he prayed about: "Sanctify them by the truth. Your word is truth" (John 17:17). Jesus is asking the Father to sanctify you and me! Isn't that wonderful?

And in this prayer, He reveals how it's going to happen: By the truth. And what is that truth? The Word of God is the truth. We read the Bible because it is God's truth, and we can only be sanctified by the truth found in God's Word.

Back to Romans 8:13. "If *by the Spirit* you put to death the misdeeds of the body, you will live." This verse also answers the question, "How do I kill sin?" Paul says that I must kill sin *by the Spirit*."

Which leads us to another well-known passage – Paul's description of the believer's armor in the battle against the world, the flesh and the devil.

"Therefore put on the full armor of God, so that when the day of evil comes, you may be able to stand your ground, and after you have done everything, to stand. Stand firm then, with *the belt of truth* buckled around your waist, with the breastplate of righteousness in place, and with your feet fitted with the readiness that comes from the gospel of peace. In addition to all this, take up the shield of faith, with which you can extinguish all the flaming arrows of the evil one. Take the helmet of salvation and *the sword of the Spirit, which is the word of God.*

The first item mentioned is "the belt of truth." And the last item is "the Sword of the Spirit, which is the word of God." God sanctifies us by His Spirit and by His Truth when we spend time in His Word. How do I defend myself when the devil sends one of his arrows in my direction? I take out my sword, my Bible, the Word of God.

Listen to what the Bible claims to be and what it is able to do for you:

"For the word of God is living and active. Sharper than any double-edged sword, it penetrates even to dividing soul and spirit, joints and marrow; it judges the thoughts and attitudes of the heart." (Hebrews 4:12)

"I have hidden your word in my heart that I might not sin against you." (Psalm 119:11)

How should we respond to our sinful nature? When our flesh beckons, we do not have to succumb. We can take out our sword and kill sin with the Word. By the power of the Spirit, we can defeat sin with the sword of the Spirit.

Jesus provides the best example of how to destroy sin with the Word. More on that in the next chapter, so read on!

SUMMARY

Reason #5: We read the Bible because it provides the power to kill sin.

Benefit: As the Spirit empowers us to remove sin, we remove the source of much pain and heartache.

Key Passages:
Mark 9:43-38
Romans 8:13
Matthew 1:21
Hebrews 12:14
John 17:17

Chapter 6:
The Bible Enables Us to Resist Temptation

Once upon a time, there was "A Man, His Dog, and a Bone." The man was training his dog to be obedient, to learn the meaning of the word "no." So the man would take a bone, or a doggie treat, and he would put the treat in the middle of the floor right next to the dog, look the dog right in the eye, and say "no."

The first time, the dog saw the treat and didn't even think twice about it. He grabbed the treat and ate it in one gulp. The master promptly came over and smacked the dog right across the face.

Then the master got out another treat and did the same thing. He put the treat in the middle of the floor, next to the dog, and once again said "no."

The dog did the same thing – saw the treat, went right for it, and swallowed it down, resulting in another hard smack across the dog's face.

So the master does it a third time – takes out a treat, puts it in the middle of the floor, and says "no." This time the dog doesn't take the treat. Instead, you know what the dog does? The dog never looks at the treat. While his master was putting the treat on the floor, the dog never for a moment took his eyes off his master. The dog knew that if I look at that treat, I'll never be able to resist the temptation, so he maintained a steadfast gaze into the eyes of his master.

Temptation is something we all experience. What is your doggie treat? What temptation have you been dealing with lately?

For some, it's a substance like alcohol or cocaine. For others, it's food consumed in excess. It could be anything from shopping to pornography.

We all have something, right? 1 Corinthians 10:13 addresses the universality of temptation. "No temptation has seized you except what is common to man."

What temptation seizes or overtakes you?

More importantly, what are you doing to resist temptation? How are you doing in your battle against temptation?

I'm here to tell you that there is hope in the struggle against sin. Regardless of what temptation you are struggling with, the Bible offers hope. Reason #6 for reading the Bible is this: the Bible enables us to resist temptation. God's Word promises us victory in the battle against temptation, and the key to that victory is found in the story about The Man, His Dog, and a Bone.

Aren't we just like the dog? When did the dog stop going for the bone? When he looked into the eyes of his master.

Likewise, the Bible teaches that the key to resisting temptation is a steadfast gaze into the face of our Master, the God-Man Jesus Christ.

Jesus faced temptation repeatedly while on earth. "Because he himself suffered when he was tempted, he is able to help those who are being tempted. For we do not have a high priest who is unable to sympathize with our weaknesses, but we have one who has been tempted in every way, just as we are – yet was without sin" (Hebrews 2:18, 4:15).

Let's take a look at Matthew 4:1-11, where we see Jesus being tempted by the devil.

"Then Jesus was led by the Spirit into the wilderness to be tempted by the devil. After fasting forty days and forty nights, he was hungry. The tempter came to him and said, "If you are the Son of God, tell these stones to become bread."

Jesus answered, "It is written: 'Man shall not live on bread alone, but on every word that comes from the mouth of God.'"

Then the devil took him to the holy city and had him stand on the highest point of the temple. "If you are the Son of God," he said, "throw yourself down. For it is written: "'He will command his angels concerning you, and they will lift you up in their hands, so that you will not strike your foot against a stone.'"

Jesus answered him, "It is also written: 'Do not put the Lord your God to the test.'"

Again, the devil took him to a very high mountain and showed him all the kingdoms of the world and their splendor. "All this I will give you," he said, "if you will bow down and worship me."

Jesus said to him, "Away from me, Satan! For it is written: 'Worship the Lord your God, and serve him only.'"

Then the devil left him, and angels came and attended him."

This passage answers the question, Why should I look to Jesus when I am tempted? I can think of three answers to that question.

Answer #1:

We should look to Jesus for victory over temptation because *Jesus is God*.

Note what Satan said in verse 3: "if you are the Son of God." The devil knew who Jesus was. The word "if" here can also be rendered "since."

Let's talk a bit about the phrase "son of God." In the Bible, this means "one who is equal to God." In John 5, after healing a man on the Sabbath, the Jewish religious leaders were upset with Jesus. "Because Jesus was doing these things on the Sabbath, the Jews persecuted him. Jesus said to them, 'My Father is always at his work to this very day, and I, too, am working.' For this reason they tried all the more to kill him; not only was he breaking the Sabbath, but he was even calling God his own Father, making himself equal with God" (John 5:16-18).

This is the teaching of Scripture: Jesus is God. John 1:1 says it so well -- "The Word was God." (See also Titus 2:13 and 1 John 5:20.) And because Jesus is God, he has the power to enable us to resist temptation. "Who is it that overcomes the world? Only he who believes that Jesus is the Son of God" (1 John 5:5).

Answer #2:

We should look to Jesus for victory over temptation because *Jesus is human*.

Back to Matthew 4. Note verse 2: "After fasting forty days and forty nights, he was hungry." Of course Jesus was hungry; He didn't eat for 40 days!

This is the teaching of Scripture: Jesus was a human being, just like you and me. He got hungry in the wilderness. He got thirsty at Jacob's well and asks the woman for a drink of water (John 4:7). He got tired because he had been walking all day (John 4:6). Jesus got so tired during the day that he'd take a nap (Mark 4:38).

Because Jesus is a man, he's been through everything you and I have been through. He's knows us inside and out, not just because He's God (and therefore knows everything), but because He lived inside a human body for 33 years.

Answer #3:

We should look to Jesus for victory over temptation because *Jesus knows the secret to resisting temptation.*

Perhaps you've seen the bumper sticker WWJD. "What Would Jesus Do?" When it comes to resisting temptation, here's an even better one: WDJD = What Did Jesus Do? What did He do when Satan tempted him?

In Matthew 4 – there are three temptations. In each temptation, Jesus did the same thing. And actually, what Jesus did was something that He said: three simple words that unlock the key to victory over temptation. "It is written" (verse 4). "It is written" (verse 7). "It is written" (verse 10).

What did Jesus do? He quoted Scripture. Jesus defeated the devil by speaking the Word of God.

The God-Man Jesus Christ memorized Bible verses. And then, when faced with temptation, He took out His Sword of the Spirit (Ephesians 6:17) and used it. The "secret" to victory in the Christian life is probably something you learned way back in Sunday school – Scripture memorization.

What do you do when faced with temptation? Are you looking to Jesus to save you from the power of sin? Or are you so fixated on the temptation that you can't see the forest from the trees.

Like the dog in our story, we must take our eyes off the temptation and look steadfastly into the face of our Master. Only Jesus can give us power to resist temptation, and we can tap into that power when we memorize Scripture and wield it as a weapon against the deceitfulness of sin.

Because He is God, only Jesus has the divine power to save us from temptation. Because He is Man, only Jesus can sympathize with our weakness and help us in our time of need. And because He knows how to use the

Word of God, only Jesus can teach us how to use the Sword of the Spirit to defeat the enemy.

SUMMARY

Reason #6: We read the Bible because it enables us to resist temptation.

Benefit: We experience the joy of victory over the enticements offered by the world, our flesh and the devil.

Key Passages:
Hebrews 2:18
Hebrews 4:15
Matthew 4:1-11

Chapter 7:
The Bible Fills Our Hearts with Joy

I love reading the Psalms. For several years now I usually start my day by reading a psalm. This simple exercise naturally leads me into a time of praise, thanksgiving and prayer. This habit has become sweet because the more time I spend reading about God's greatness, the more I want to worship Him. And the more I worship King Jesus, the more content I am. We were made to adore our Creator. And when I do what I was made to do, life is good!

There are many words I could use to describe what I experience during these early morning praise sessions. I already mentioned being "content." Another would be "joyful." "Joy" is a rich word that is used repeatedly in the psalms. "Joy" and its related words (like "joyful" and "rejoice") appear in the Psalms about 100 times! When I read a psalm and worship Jesus, I am filled with joy. It's a beautiful thing. Certainly the intensity of my joy can vary from day to day. But over the past few years, I can honestly say that God has been increasing my joy. And I believe this is a direct result of spending time in the psalms, focusing on His majesty and splendor.

Here are some of my thoughts on joy that come directly from the Psalms.

1. Biblical joy can be defined and described by looking at several other words the psalmists use in close proximity to joy.

Gladness

Of all the words used to accompany "joy," this one is used most often.

"But let all who take refuge in you be glad; let them every sing for joy" (Psalm 5:11)

"I will be glad and rejoice in you" (Psalm 9:2)

"Therefore my heart is glad and my tongue rejoices" (Psalm 16:9)

"Surely you have granted him unending blessings and made him glad with the joy of your presence" (Psalm 21:6)

"I will be glad and rejoice in your love" (Psalm 31:7)

"Rejoice in the Lord and be glad, you righteous" (Psalm 32:11)

"But may all who seek you rejoice and be glad in you" (Psalm 40:16 and 70:4)

Delight

"Then my soul will rejoice in the LORD and delight in his salvation" (Psalm 35:9)

"Then I will go to the altar of God, to God, my joy and my delight" (Psalm 43:4)

Pleasure

"You will fill me with joy in your presence, with eternal pleasures at your right hand" (Psalm 16:11)

Satisfaction

"Satisfy us in the morning with your unfailing love, that we may sing for joy and be glad all our days" (Psalm 90:14)

Celebration

"They rejoice in your name all day long; they celebrate your righteousness" (Psalm 89:16)

"They celebrate your abundant goodness and joyfully sing of your righteousness" (Psalm 145:7)

2. The source of biblical joy is God and God alone. He provides it; it is His gift to us.

"You make known to me the path of life; you will fill me with joy in your presence, with eternal pleasures at your right hand (Psalm 16:11)

"You turned my wailing into dancing; you removed my sackcloth and clothed me with joy" (Psalm 30:11)

3. Biblical joy is experienced when we worship God for who God is (His attributes, such as His love) and what He does (His miraculous deeds on our behalf, especially His salvation).

The psalmists often express and experience joy as the direct result of praising God for His matchless character or His mighty works (or both).

"But may all who seek you rejoice and be glad in you; may those who long for your saving help always say, 'The LORD is great!' (Psalm 40:16)

"I will be glad and rejoice in your love, for you saw my affliction and knew the anguish of my soul" (Psalm 31:7)

"They rejoice in your name all day long; they celebrate your righteousness" (Psalm 89:16)

"Satisfy us in the morning with your unfailing love, that we may sing for joy and be glad all our days" (Psalm 90:14)

"They celebrate your abundant goodness and joyfully sing of your righteousness" (Psalm 145:7)

"I may declare your praises in the gates of Daughter Zion, and there rejoice in your salvation" (Psalm 9:15)

"But I trust in your unfailing love; my heart rejoices in your salvation" (Psalm 13:5)

"Then my soul will rejoice in the LORD and delight in his salvation" (Psalm 35:9)

"Restore to me the joy of your salvation and grant me a willing spirit" (Psalm 51:12)

"He turned the sea into dry land, they passed through the waters on foot— come, let us rejoice in him" (Psalm 66:6)

"My lips will shout for joy when I sing praise to you— I whom you have delivered" (Psalm 71:23)

"For you make me glad by your deeds, LORD; I sing for joy at what your hands have done" (Psalm 92:4)

"Let them sacrifice thank offerings and tell of his works with songs of joy" (Psalm 107:22)

"Shouts of joy and victory resound in the tents of the righteous: The LORD's right hand has done mighty things!" (Psalm 118:15)

4. The most common description of biblical joy in the psalms is simply "joy in God." This phrase appears at least ten times in the psalms.

"Those who love your name may rejoice in you" (Psalm 5:11)

"I will be glad and rejoice in you" (Psalm 9:2; see also Psalm 70:4)

"Rejoice in the LORD" (Psalm 32:11)

"In him our hearts rejoice" (Psalm 33:21)

"Then my soul will rejoice in the LORD" (PSALM 35:9)

"But may all who seek you rejoice and be glad in you" (Psalm 40:16)

"But the king will rejoice in God" (Psalm 63:11)

"The righteous will rejoice in the LORD" (PSALM 64:10)

"Come, let us rejoice in him" (Psalm 66:6)

"Will you not revive us again, that your people may rejoice in you?" (Psalm 85:6)

A similar phrase to "joy in God" is "joy in the presence of God."

"You will fill me with joy in your presence, with eternal pleasures at your right hand" (Psalm 16:11)

"Surely you have granted him unending blessings and made him glad with the joy of your presence" (Psalm 21:6)

Isn't the Word of God amazing! We can learn so much from doing a word study like the one just presented. Sometimes it's best to let the Word speak for itself. Reading these verses about joy in rapid succession is a wonderful way to allow God to teach us His truth directly from the Scriptures.

With this word study in mind, we can describe biblical joy as the intense, celebratory feelings of gladness, delight, pleasure and satisfaction that come from God Himself as we focus on His glorious character and His mighty deeds of salvation performed on our behalf. Furthermore, biblical joy is the blissful wonder and awe we experience when we are consciously aware of His presence. For the Christian, joy in God is available at all times, in any situation. By definition, joy in Him can be found regardless of our circumstances. As Paul wrote, we can even be "sorrowful, yet always rejoicing" (2 Corinthians 6:10).

Now I'd like to turn our attention to two other verses that answer the question: "What can I do to increase my biblical joy?" Perhaps you are wondering about this yourself. Our emotions can be all over the map on any given day, right? And when we talk about biblical joy, we're not saying that God expects us to be in a state of giddiness 24/7. Life is filled with heartache and disappointment, and Christians have just as much sadness as non-Christians. "Yet man is born to trouble as surely as sparks fly upward" (Job 5:7). Jesus did not promise us a problem-free life. Rather, He promised us a life of difficulty. "In this world you will have trouble" (John 16:33).

But as 2 Corinthians 6:10 teaches, we can have biblical joy (that deep sense of satisfaction and contentment in God no matter what happens) in the midst of sorrow because our joy is found in Him. How do we experience that kind of joy? Here's how.

"The precepts of the LORD are right, giving joy to the heart. The commands of the LORD are radiant, giving light to the eyes" (Psalm 19:8).

"Your statutes are my heritage forever; they are the joy of my heart" (Psalm 119:111).

Earlier we read many verses that clearly portray God as the source of our joy. Psalm 43:4 is one of my favorites in this regard: "Then I will go to the altar of God, my joy and my delight" (Psalm 43:4). Here the psalmist says God is not just the source of my joy, He is my joy. He is my delight!

Then we read Psalm 19:8 and we hear the psalmist saying that the Word is the source of my joy. Psalm 119:111 goes even further and teaches that the Word is my joy. Which is it? Is God my joy, or is the Word my joy?

The answer, of course, is both. God and His word are my source of joy. God and His Word are the joy of my heart. This is a teaching found throughout Scripture: God and His Word are described interchangeably.

SUMMARY

Reason #7: We read the Bible because it fills our hearts with joy.

Benefit: We experience biblical joy, the joy provided by God Almighty regardless of our circumstances.

Key Passages:
Psalm 5:11
Psalm 35:9
Psalm 16:11
Psalm 90:14
Psalm 89:16
Psalm 40:16
Psalm 19:8

Chapter 8:
The Bible Brings Us into God's Presence

Over the past few years I've become increasingly obsessed with God. I have this ever-growing desire to know Him and to be with Him. I want to understand Him as He really is.

Now I realize we can never know God fully. We're finite little creatures with pea-sized brains and a natural inclination to rebel against God. I'm well aware of my own sinful nature every day. I am "prone to wander, Lord, I feel it; prone to leave the God I love."

Amazingly, even though our love for Him can vary from day to day, God is relentlessly faithful in His pursuit to make Himself known to us. He desires a relationship of intimacy, devotion, love and obedience. And I long for that.

Then there's the simple fact that God is so much bigger and stronger and smarter than us. He's God! And we're not. So how do we bridge this massive gulf between the infinite and the finite?

My answer to that question is this: we go the one resource that claims to reveal God in all His glory – the

Bible. We go to the written Word of God to find the living God.

With those thoughts in mind, here's a question: How do you describe God? Let's brainstorm and make a list of all the words that come to mind when you think about God. I'll go first. Ready? God is . . .

Righteous
Wonderful
Life-preserving
Strength-giving
Delightful
Good
Trustworthy
Precious
Eternal
Enduring
Boundless
Omnipresent
Insightful
Understanding
Sweet
Light-giving
Joy-giving
Peace-giving
Hope-giving
Saving

Well, that's a start. I could go on and on. And I'm sure you could, too. Undoubtedly my list contains words that resonate with your heart and mind. And I'm sure my list omitted one or more of your favorite words to describe God.

Again, I don't want to minimize the fact that there's a sense in which God is indescribable and undefinable. At the same time, God has seen fit to use language to communicate to us, so I have no problem with this exercise. Sure, human words can only scratch the surface in our attempt to mine the depths of God's greatness. But it is the medium God has chosen to disclose Himself to us. So let's take advantage of it, to the best of our ability, while realizing that our understanding of God is but a drop in the bucket. Or better said, a drop in the ocean or a grain of sand on the seashore.

Here's where I'm going with this. All the words in my list come from Psalm 119, the longest chapter in the Bible. I've come to love this psalm. It is a treasure chest of divine truth, with 176 verses divided into 22 stanzas of 8 verses each. And virtually every verse in this psalm teaches us something about the Word of God.

Yes, the longest chapter in the Bible is all about the Bible. Certainly there is much in this psalm about God. And there is also much in Psalm 119 about the writer, for he shares many details about his difficult life; he is experiencing much stress and is facing intense persecution from people who hate him.

But when you read this psalm you will be amazed at the writer's devotion to and obsession with God's Word. In fact, the 20 adjectives in my list above are all used by the writer of Psalm 119 to describe the Word of God, not God! This simple fact intrigues me to no end.

Here are the 20 verses from which I formulated my list:

I will praise you with an upright heart as I learn your *righteous* laws (Psalm 119:7)

Open my eyes that I may see *wonderful* things in your law (Psalm 119:18)

I am laid low in the dust; *preserve* my life according to your word (Psalm 119:25)

My soul is weary with sorrow; *strengthen* me according to your word (Psalm 119:28)

Your statutes are my *delight*; they are my counselors (Psalm 119:24)

Take away the disgrace I dread, for your laws are *good* (Psalm 119:39)

I *trust* in your word (Psalm 119:42)

The law from your mouth is more *precious* to me than thousands of pieces of silver and gold (Psalm 119:72)

Your word, Lord, is *eternal*; it stands firm in the heavens (Psalm 119:89)

Your laws *endure* to this day, for all things serve you (Psalm 119:91)

To all perfection I see a limit, but your commands are *boundless* (Psalm 119:96)

Your commands are *always with me* and make me wiser than my enemies (Psalm 119:98)

I have more *insight* than all my teachers, for I meditate on your statutes (Psalm 119:99)

I have more *understanding* than the elders, for I obey your precepts (Psalm 119:100)

How *sweet* are your words to my taste, sweeter than honey to my mouth (Psalm 119:103)

Your word is a lamp for my feet, a *light* on my path (Psalm 119:105)

Your statutes are my heritage forever; they are the *joy* of my heart (Psalm 119:111)

Great *peace* have those who love your law, and nothing can make them stumble (Psalm 119:165)

I rise before dawn and cry for help; I have put my *hope* in your word (Psalm 119:147)

May your unfailing love come to me, Lord, your *salvation*, according to your promise (Psalm 119:41)

These 20 statements are a small sample of the dozens of verses in Psalm 119 that describe the Word of God in terms that are also used elsewhere in Scripture to describe God. Do you think we could find a verse in the Bible that says "God is righteous." Of course! There's plenty of them. "Answer me when I call to you, O my righteous God" (Psalm 4:1). Or how about this one: "For the Lord is righteous, he loves justice" (Psalm 11:7).

In Psalm 7, David is consumed with God's righteousness. He mentions it repeatedly. "God is a righteous judge, a God who expresses his wrath every day . . . I will give thanks to the Lord because of His righteousness and will sing praise to the name of the Lord Most High" (Psalm 7:11, 17).

How about "wonderful." God's Word is wonderful and so the psalmist prays to see "wonderful things" in the Word (Psalm 119:18). Is God wonderful? Absolutely. Can you think of a verse that uses that word to describe God? Here's one. "For to us a child is born, to us a son is given, and the government will be on his shoulders. And he will be called Wonderful, Counselor, Mighty God, Everlasting Father, Prince of Peace" (Isaiah 9:6).

We could continue through the list, finding verses that describe God as good and delightful and trustworthy and eternal and omnipresent and so on. You would expect this, wouldn't you? This is why Paul told Timothy, "from infancy you have known the *holy* Scriptures" (2 Timothy 3:15). Because the Word comes from God, and God is holy, His Word must also be holy. The Word of God is a reflection of the character of God.

Let me now state Reason #8 for reading the Bible: We read the Bible because it brings us into the presence of God. Since the Word of God is as holy as God Himself, reading His Word is equivalent to having a face-to-face conversation with Him. He communicates to us through the pages of Scripture, and we communicate to Him through praise, thanksgiving, worship and prayer.

In any relationship, if you want to get to know the other person, what must happen? You must spend much time with that person, and that person must open up his heart to you and communicate.

Have you ever wondered why the Bible is such a long book – over a thousand pages! I think He gave us so much to read because He has so much to say. And He has so much to say because He wants us to spend as much time as possible in His presence, listening to Him and learning from Him, cultivating a love relationship of deep intimacy. Such a relationship can only develop when both parties are communicating with one another.

And the benefit of being in the presence of God by reading Scripture is breathtaking, isn't it? If you've read this far, I'm confident that you share my passion to know God intimately, being satisfied to simply sit at His feet and listen. The psalmist captures the essence of the wonder of His presence:

"One thing I ask of the Lord, this is what I seek: that I may dwell in the house of the Lord all the days of my life, to gaze upon the beauty of the Lord and to seek him in his temple" (Psalm 27:4).

When we read the Bible, we can sit at the feet of Jesus and gaze upon His beauty with the eyes of faith. We are caught up in the splendor of His majesty, "filled with an inexpressible and glorious joy" (1 Peter 1:8) as we experience the deepest communion a human being can possibly have, doing what we were made to do, living in the light our Creator and being satisfied in Him simply because we are with Him.

SUMMARY

Reason #8: We read the Bible because it brings us into the very presence of God.

Benefit: Our relationship with Him grows more intimate and our worship of Him becomes more biblically informed.

Key Passages:

Psalm 119:7

Psalm 119:18

Psalm 119:25

Psalm 119:28

Psalm 119:24

Psalm 119:39

Psalm 119:42

Psalm 119:72

Psalm 119:89

Psalm 119:91

Psalm 119:96

Psalm 119:98

Psalm 119:99

Psalm 119:100

Psalm 119:103

Psalm 119:105

Psalm 119:111

Psalm 119:165

Psalm 119:147

Psalm 119:41

Chapter 9:
The Bible Gives Freedom

What I remember most about her room was the smell -- a strange mixture of incense, smoke and alcohol.

I rarely went into my sister's bedroom, but one day circa 1972 I was compelled to do so.

I had recently made a profession of faith in Jesus. As a high school freshman I had heard the gospel by attending a Baptist church with a good friend. I had been reading the Bible daily and was learning much about Christianity.

Meanwhile, my sister, two years older, was spending time with a different crowd. Substance abuse was the activity of choice for her and her friends. Drugs and alcohol had become her constant companion. And I could see the effect this was having on her. She was seldom sober.

I had to do something. So I picked up a Bible and knocked on her door. She told me to come in. As I sat down on the couch directly across from her bed, I looked at her and could see the dazed look in her eyes. She was, as we said back then, stoned.

I asked her: "Is this the kind of life you want to live?"

I don't remember what she might have said in response. Probably nothing. But I knew she could hear me. Even people in a coma can hear you. It didn't matter what state was in. All I knew was that the Book in my hand contained the message that could liberate her from this prison she was in. She was a slave who needed to be set free.

I opened my Bible and turned to John chapter 3. I read the story of Jesus and Nicodemus. I read John 3:16 to her. And then I said, "You need a new life. You need to be born again."

Then I gave her the Bible and left. I don't know how long I was there. Maybe 5 or 10 minutes max.

Do you believe in the power of the gospel? Do you believe that God can save anyone, no matter what they've done or what condition they are in? No matter how depressed or how drunk or how angry or how depressed or how violent?

I do. I believe God can save anybody, anytime, anywhere. Only one thing is needed: the Word of God must be present. The message of the gospel must be communicated in some way, shape or form, and then the Holy Spirit can take over and come into a person's heart and change them from the inside out, granting the gift of repentance and saving faith, and in the process of doing that, He forgives all their sin and sets them free from both the penalty and power of sin.

I believe that God can save anybody because the Bible says so. "Then they cried to the Lord in their trouble, and he saved them from their distress. He brought them out of darkness and the deepest gloom and broke away their chains. Let them give thanks to the Lord for his unfailing love and his wonderful deeds for men, for he breaks gates of bronze and cuts through bars of iron" (Psalm 107:14-16).

I believe that God can save anybody because He saved me. Watching my sister's life deteriorate before my eyes was enough negative reinforcement for me to stay away from alcohol and drugs. But I am just as much a sinner as my sister. I needed forgiveness of sins just as much as she did. (You can read the story of how God saved me in my book, "The Ultimate Communicator: One Man's Search for the Meaning of Life.")

Certainly my sister's conversion experience is, in some ways, more dramatic than mine. But God didn't liberate her on the day I entered her room and gave her a Bible. A few years later, however, while watching a TV evangelist, she heard the gospel again and suddenly remembered, "That's what Wayne was trying to tell me."

Do you ever wonder whether people can be set free from sin by watching television? Yes, God can even save someone while watching TV, because that's what happened to my sister. While hearing the gospel on television, she committed her life to Christ and started reading the Bible I gave her, which she had kept. It hasn't been easy, but my sister is no longer a substance abuser. God has freed her from the grip of drugs and alcohol, and she lives for Jesus today.

In 2006, some 34 years after I shared the gospel with my sister, she sent me a birthday card and wrote these words:

"Wayne, I love you so much. Thank you for planting the seeds of the Word of the gospel, especially John 3:16, back when we were in high school. I can to this day remember the awesome witness you gave me. Your boldness saved me from eternal hell. I can't wait to worship our Lord forever."

More Thoughts On Freedom

NOTE: The following is an excerpt from my book, "Sweeter Than Honey, More Precious Than Gold: Meditations on Psalm 119."

When I think about what God did for my sister, I can't help but think of what the Bible says about freedom. For the Christian, every day is Independence Day when you read a verse like Psalm 119:45 -- "I will walk about in freedom, for I have sought out your precepts."

We treasure our freedom, do we not? In the USA, we sing proudly before every sporting event that we live in "the land of the free and the home of the brave."

I'm thankful for the frequent reminders that freedom is not free; it comes at a great price. The freedom we enjoy in this country is the result of much blood, sweat and tears.

The psalmist speaks of his life as a life of freedom. Literally, the first half of Psalm 119:45 can be translated, "I shall walk in a wide place" (ESV). Isn't that a wonderful way to describe the meaning of liberty?

What I find most compelling about this verse is the relationship between the first half and the second half. Note the all-important connecting word -- "for" - which means "because". The psalmist says he lives in freedom, and then he tells us the reason for that freedom. He has freedom because he seeks out the Word of God.

Like our blood-bought freedom as U.S. citizens, the believer's freedom is not free. It too comes at a price. The freedom of the believer is the result of seeking God's truth and finding it in the written Word of God, the Bible.

Once we have sought out and found God's Word, we must spend much time reading it, studying it, meditating on it, understanding it, memorizing it, and obeying it - all by the grace of God, empowered by the Spirit of God.

This is what it takes to experience the life of freedom - God's freedom.

Now let's turn our attention to the question, "Freedom from what?" The answer to this question is found in one of the Bible's major themes - liberation from the slavery of sin.

Jesus described the human condition brilliantly and succinctly: "Everyone who sins is a slave to sin" (John 8:34). That is our plight. We are in bondage to sin, for who can exclude himself/herself from the "everyone" of Christ's indictment?

Because of our sin, we are slaves to the ugly consequences of sin in both this life and the next. The Bible is oh so clear about this: as sinners, the death sentence of hell is hanging over our heads (the ultimate penalty of sin - see Romans 6:23). Before God rescues us from the kingdom of darkness, we stand at the precipice of eternity, with nothing below but the lake of fire.

And we live every day battling temptation on every side. Apart from the grace of God, we are doomed to succumb to the forces of evil that entice us (the pervading power of sin - see Ephesians 2:1-3).

Is there any hope for us to escape the penalty and power of sin?

Yes! This is one of the many reasons that the gospel about Jesus Christ is good news! Freedom from sin is found in Jesus. He came to liberate us from slavery to sin.

Listen to these words, spoken by Jesus himself when he visited his hometown of Nazareth and read Isaiah 61:1-2 in the synagogue --

"He (God) has sent me (Jesus) to proclaim freedom for the prisoners and recovery of sight for the blind, to release the oppressed, to proclaim the year of the Lord's favor" (Luke 4:18-19).

This was the definitive pronouncement of the Mission Statement of Jesus. He came to set us free from the prison of sin. He came to release us from both its penalty and power.

And he accomplished this mission when he died on the cross, for his death paid the penalty of sin and unleashed God's power into the lives of every person who embraces him as Savior, Lord and Treasure.

This is the freedom that we enjoy as blood-bought believers in Jesus Christ. And this freedom is found by seeking and finding the Great Liberator as he is revealed in the pages of God's holy Word. May we never stop praising our King for setting us free, for when we know the truth, both written and incarnate, "the truth will set you free" (John 8:32).

SUMMARY

<u>Reason #9:</u> We read the Bible because it sets us free!

<u>Benefit:</u> Freedom from sin's vice-like grip of slavery.

<u>Key Passages:</u>
Psalm 11:45
John 8:32-34
Luke 4:18:19

Chapter 10:
The Bible Leads Us to Jesus

Jesus made some amazing statements. He claimed to be God, and He did so repeatedly. "I tell you the truth, before Abraham was born, I am." The Jewish religious leaders were so outraged at this blatant pronouncement of deity that "they picked up stones to stone him." But it wasn't time for Him to die, so "Jesus hid himself, slipping away" from their grasp (John 8:58-59).

Here's another bold statement Jesus made to the religious establishment, men who spent years studying and teaching the Old Testament. "You diligently study the Scriptures because you think that by them you possess eternal life. These are the Scriptures that testify about me, yet you refuse to come to me to have life" (John 5:39-40).

"These are the Scriptures that testify about me."

I think it's difficult if not impossible for us to grasp just how radical this statement would have sounded to a first century Jew steeped in the traditions of ancient Judaism. Not only did Jesus claim to be God, He claimed to be the Messiah, the One spoken about throughout the Old Testament as "the anointed one," the long-awaited King who would come to save His people from their enemies and establish the kingdom of God on earth. He was saying, in effect, that "I am the One prophesied by the prophets of old."

And here's one more audacious claim:

"I am the way and the truth and the life. No one comes to the Father except through me" (John 14:6).

This was an astonishing statement in any era. It was a hard pill to swallow 2,000 years ago. And it's a hard pill to swallow today. In our age of religious tolerance, many people today find fault with such a narrow-minded perspective.

For orthodox Christians, however, it is one of our most treasured Scriptures. The purpose of this chapter is to explain the meaning of this verse and to see how it supports Reason #10: We read the Bible because it leads us to Jesus, and Jesus takes us to God.

First, let's get the context. Asking simple questions is a good way to see how any one verse fits into the bigger picture.

Who said this? Jesus.

Who is he addressing? The apostles.

When and where did he say this? On the night before his crucifixion, Jesus and his disciples were celebrating the Passover meal in the Upper Room. This scene is also known as the Last Supper because it is Jesus' final meal with his closest followers before being arrested, tried and killed on Good Friday.

Perhaps the most important question is: *Why* did Jesus say this? John 14:6 is Jesus' answer to a question. More on that in a moment.

Jesus has been preparing the disciples for his departure. Note John 13:33, "My children, I will be with you only a little longer. You will look for me, and just as I told the Jews, so I tell you now: Where I am going, you cannot come." Then in verse 36 Peter asks, "Lord, where are you going?" Jesus replied, "Where I am going, you cannot follow now, but you will follow later."

Jesus knows that he will be crucified the next day and is doing his best to get the disciples ready for this. His inevitable death has been a topic of discussion during the final months of his 3-year ministry. Mark's gospel records Jesus' straightforward prediction. In no uncertain terms, Jesus has been telling them, "We're going to Jerusalem, and I'm going to be killed there. And three days later I will rise from the dead." (See Mark 8:31-33, Mark 9:30-32 and Mark 10:32-34.)

The disciples do not know what to make of this. Even though Jesus "spoke plainly" about it, on one occasion "Peter took him aside and began to rebuke him" (Mark 8:32). Their confusion is to be expected, of course, given all that Jesus has said and done in their presence. Mark provides insightful commentary on these exchanges: "But they did not understand what he meant and were afraid to ask him about it" (Mark 9:32).

So now we've come to the 13th hour in the Upper Room and Jesus once again brings up his departure. "In my Father's house are many rooms . . . I am going there to prepare a place for you" (John 14:2).

Then Thomas says, "Lord, we don't know where you are going, so how can we know the way?" (John 14:5).

Jesus answers this question with his famous words, "I am the way and the truth and the life. No one comes to the Father except through me" (John 14:6).

With our 20/20 hindsight, it's easy for us to wonder about Thomas and his question. Jesus has just said, "I am going there to prepare a place for you" (John 14:2). Where is he going? To "my Father's house" (v.2). And later he says, "I am going to the Father" (v.12).

But Thomas and his companions are like a deer caught in the headlights. They just don't get it. Again, let's not be too hard on them. Would we have reacted any differently?

In the midst of the apostles' confusion, Jesus is presenting some of the most compelling and comforting teaching in the Bible. In a word, they are "troubled" (John 14:1).

Their leader is telling them that he is leaving soon, and he is providing words to help them deal with the shock of his departure.

It is in this context that Jesus says "I am the way" to God the Father and the heavenly house that he inhabits. Much has been written and said about heaven. This passage contains one of the most beautiful descriptions of the Christian's eternal abode – heaven is "my Father's house" (John 14:2).

Is this not a wonderful metaphor? Think for a moment about this: If you are believer in Jesus Christ, you will live forever in your Father's house! What is heaven like? For the Christian, it is home. It's where you belong. It's that one place where safety and security abound without measure.

Reflect on the many pleasant characteristics of your own home, and multiply that description by infinity, and you're now getting a picture of what heaven will be like. Breathtaking, isn't it?

And what makes it all possible? It is the house of *God.* It is the presence of the Lord Almighty, Creator of heaven and earth, that makes heaven such a glorious place. When we ponder the delights of eternity, this should be our focus, because this was Jesus' focus.

Jesus said, "I am the way." The way to where? "I am the way . . . No one comes *to the Father* except through me" (John 14:6). And a few sentences later he says, "I am going *to the Father"* (John 14:12). For Jesus, going back to heaven meant going back *to the Father*.

Ah, but there's more!

Jesus also says that the way to the Father is *"through me"* (John 14:6). Jesus was leaving the apostles, but this separation was temporary. He promised to come back and "take you *to be with me* that you may also be *where I am"* (John 14:3).

Heaven is not only our Father's house, it is also the place where Jesus will live forever. When we go to heaven, we are going to live with the Father *and* the Son. Could there be a more precious promise in all of Scripture than this!

Scripture abounds with mind-boggling descriptions of heaven. It is a home unlike any we've experienced on earth. It is a place where "There will be no more death or mourning or crying or pain" (Revelation 21:4). We can only imagine the glory of heaven! It is so glorious that the apostle Paul was "caught up to Paradise" but not allowed to talk about it. "He heard inexpressible things, things that man is not permitted to tell" (2 Corinthians 12:2-4).

But heaven is our hope. And so we should think about it, long for it, and serve God patiently while waiting for it.

Jesus' comments about heaven remind me of a question I first heard in a John Piper sermon. "Why do you want to go to heaven?"

I had never thought of such a question before. What is my motive for going there?

Imagine you could go to heaven and receive all the promised benefits. No more sickness or death. No more suffering. No more sorrow. You get to live forever in a perfect environment, with all the comforts of home multiplied a million times.

You get to experience everything the Bible says about heaven, with one exception. Jesus is not there.

Do you still want to go?

If Jesus is not in heaven, do you still want to go to there?

Think about it today. And examine yourself in the light of John 14:3. "If I go and prepare a place for you, I will come back and take you *to be with me* that you may also be where I am."

When Jesus talked about heaven, the emphasis was *being with him*. That is the main attraction of heaven -- Jesus. Should that not be our main reason for desiring heaven?

May it be so.

May we say with Paul, "I desire to depart and be with Christ, which is better by far" (Philippians 1:23). May we long for heaven because we long to be "at home with the Lord" (2 Corinthians 5:8).

As we conclude this study of ten wonderful reasons to read the Bible, I pray that you'll be filled with thankfulness for the Word. Without it, how would we know that Jesus is the way to the one true God?

SUMMARY:

Reason #10: We read the Bible because it leads us to Jesus, and Jesus leads us to God.

Benefit: We get to be with Jesus today, tomorrow, and forever.

Key Passages:
John 8:58-59
John 5:35-40
John 14:1-14
Philippians 1:23
2 Corinthians 5:8

Conclusion

Here's a recap of the Top 10 Reasons to read the Bible today.

Reason #1

We read the Bible because it is the inspired Word of God and therefore has authority over our lives.

Benefit: Countless blessings and the rewards of living in obedience to the will of God.

Reason #2

We read the Bible because it teaches us God's way of salvation.

Benefit: In this life, we can be saved from the penalty and power of sin; in the next life, we will be saved from the presence of sin. Salvation from sin and all its consequences in both this life and the next.

Reason #3

We read the Bible because it strengthens our faith.

Benefit: The contentment of living a God-pleasing life, because "without faith, it is impossible to please God" (Hebrews 11:6).

Reason #4

We read the Bible because it leads us on the path of increasing godliness – "The Changing Life."

Benefit: As we grow spiritually, by the grace and power of God we become stronger and better able to handle whatever happens in life.

Reason #5

We read the Bible because it provides the power to kill sin.

Benefit: As the Spirit empowers us to remove sin, we remove the source of much pain and heartache.

Reason #6

We read the Bible because it enables us to resist temptation.

Benefit: We experience the joy of victory over the enticements offered by the world, our flesh and the devil.

Reason #7

We read the Bible because it fills our hearts with joy.

Benefit: We experience biblical joy, the joy provided by God Almighty regardless of our circumstances.

Reason #8

We read the Bible because it brings us into the very presence of God.

Benefit: Our relationship with Him grows more intimate and our worship of Him becomes more biblically informed.

Reason #9

We read the Bible because it sets us free!

Benefit: Freedom from sin's vice-like grip of slavery.

Reason #10

We read the Bible because it leads us to Jesus, and Jesus leads us to God.

Benefit: We get to be with Jesus today, tomorrow, and forever.

About the Author

WAYNE DAVIES lives in Fort Wayne, Indiana. He is a graduate of Grace College (B.A. in Biblical Studies) and Columbia International University (M.A. in Theology). He enjoys reading, walking and being with his family.

Wayne is President of Good Messengers Ministries of Fort Wayne, an evangelical ministry dedicated to equipping Christians to communicate the Biblical gospel. For more information, visit www.Good-Messengers.com.

Looking for more Bible reading tips? For a free copy of Wayne's Resource Guide, "Top 5 Free Online Bible Study Tools", visit www.GodWroteTheBook.com

For more information on Wayne's books, including how to purchase print copies, please visit www.GodWroteTheBook.com/books

You are welcome to contact Wayne directly with your comments or questions at wayne@GodWroteTheBook.com.

One Last Thing

If you enjoyed this book or found it useful I'd be very grateful if you'd post a short review on Amazon. Your support really does make a difference and I read all the reviews personally so I can get your feedback and make this book even better.

If you'd like to leave a review please visit this book's page on Amazon and scroll down to "Customer Reviews." Here's the link:

http://www.amazon.com/dp/B010VU9APE/

For a complete list of my books, please visit my Amazon.com Author Page here:

www.amazon.com/author/waynedavies

Thanks again for your support!

Made in the USA
San Bernardino, CA
04 July 2020